This book is dedicated to all who find Nature not an adversary to conquer and destroy, but a storehouse of infinite knowledge and experience linking man to all things past and present. They know conserving the natural environment is essential to our future well-being.

HALEAKALĀ
THE STORY BEHIND THE SCENERY®

by Jennifer M. Talken-Spaulding

Jennifer Talken-Spaulding has served the National Park Service for many years in interpretation, cultural resources management and public affairs. Her career spans over eight National Park areas, with nearly five years at Haleakalā. Jennifer has a broad appreciation and love for the resources of the national park system.

Haleakalā National Park, *located on the island of Maui, Hawai'i, was established in 1916 to preserve outstanding scenic, geological and biological resources and native Hawaiian cultural values.*

Front cover: Silversword and Haleakalā Crater; photo by Larry Ulrich. Inside front cover: Kīpahulu costal area; photo by Bob Butterfield. Page 1: Nēnē. Hawaiian Goose family; photo by Jack Jeffery.
Pages 2/3: Fog shrouded cinder cones; photo by David Muench.

Edited by Maryellen Conner. Book design by K. C. DenDooven.

Nineth Printing, Revised Edition, 2003

Clouds weaving in and around the summit cinder cones of Haleakalā carry whispers of another time. It is said that the demigod Māui fished Haleakalā and all Hawaiian volcanoes

DAVID MUENCH

from the sea, pulling them up and flinging his fishhook to the heavens. On clear nights, the fishhook of Māui, now called Scorpio, can still be seen in the sky from the summit of Haleakalā.

Haleakalā is one-half of the island of Maui and a link in a chain of remote volcanic islands stretching for miles in the wide Pacific Ocean. Everything that comes to Haleakalā is united in a single fact; it takes a journey to get here. Once here, nothing and no one can go away unchanged.

The solitude of Haleakalā has taken in plants, birds and insects that, quietly over the ages, have become new species. Ancient lava landscapes have weathered and colored over time as winds and rains oxidized earthly elements. Young black lava turned red with iron, yellow with sulfur, or the lighter browns that come with age. People, settling on the shores of Haleakalā, have grown crops, children and lives rich with the natural beauty of this place.

Haleakalā holds something different for everyone. Whether it is a cloud coated rainforest walk or an alpine hike with a view for miles, Haleakalā is rich in resources that call to each of us.

***A** hiker enjoys a quiet walk* through the wilderness of Haleakalā *where over thirty miles of trail winds* through a changing landscape of *color and contrast.*

The Haleakalā Story

PETER FRENCH

Haleakalā is known around the world for its rocky red summit shown in contrast to its strange and spiky, silvery plants. Haleakalā National Park is the number one tourist destination on Maui, but coming here is more than just a visit to check off a "to do" list.

Haleakalā offers space and quiet, diverse scenery and stories for both *malihini* (newcomers) and *kama'āina* (native-born). Those who take the time to stay a little longer begin to realize there's more to Haleakalā than meets the eye.

A visit to Haleakalā at any season offers something special. In this tropical environment, winters bring nourishing rains and plants green, bloom, and fruit. Waterfalls are full and streams run swiftly. At the summit, any early morning may bring chilling cold and occasionally frost, ice or even snow. Summers are drier, days just a little longer, and skies a little bluer. Nighttime above the clouds offers an uninterrupted 360-degree view of spectacular stars.

Visitors emerging from the mixed alien pine forest at the park entrance to the summit area are greeted to a visual blanket of rare Hawaiian plants. After miles on a windy road, the view of Haleakalā Crater before you reveals the heart and source of all that now lives on Haleakalā.

Those who drive the twisty Hāna Highway to the coastal part of the park discover that there are few sweeter smells than the forests of Kīpahulu after a rain.

Haleakalā stands tall, and sits broadly in the Pacific Ocean. It holds an unparalleled diversity of life and a long human history. A few steps in and you too become a part of the Haleakalā story.

A spur trail off the Sliding Sands trail leads to *Ka Lu'u o ka 'Ō'ō* the only cinder cone in the park that has a trail to its rim. The Class 1 air quality found at Haleakalā allows hikers and sightseers to take a long look over miles of land or out to sea.

*T*he subtle sweetness of 'ōhelo berries are a tasty treat for hikers, especially along the Halemau'u Trail in the summit area. *Nēnē* (Hawaiian goose) also enjoy these colorful fruits.

BOB BUTTERFIELD

*W*ater feeds the forests on the southeastern slopes of Haleakalā. Native plants absorb and process the water that filters through streams, falls and aquifers, sustaining all life on Haleakalā. Hikers to Waimoku Falls in Kīpahulu have the opportunity to experience this interaction first hand. The two-hour journey winds through a mixed forest of native and alien plants on a trail that is often muddy. Knowing hikers enjoy the 400' (122 m) waterfall from a distance as boulders and logs sometimes make the trip over the waterfall's edge along with the stream.

LAURENCE PARENT

" …there are few **sweeter** smells than the **forests** of **Kīpahulu** after a **rain**. "

Maui, the second youngest island...
has started on an erosional journey that will end
only when the island is returned to the sea
from which it emerged.

Building a Foundation for Life

BRAD LEWIS

"The crater floor was like another world, its cinder cones and lava a colorful mix of reds, browns, yellows and blacks."
--Horace Albright, second Director of the National Park Service on his 1920 hike in Haleakalā.

If it were not for the power of volcanoes, none of the life we enjoy on the Hawaiian Islands would exist; indeed, the islands themselves would not exist. These islands are volcanoes, massive mountains created over millions of years of volcanic activity. Their valleys and shorter summits to the northwest of the island chain are the result of thousands of years of erosion. Lying near the southeastern end of the Hawaiian archipelago, Haleakalā is an intermediate stage volcano in a complex, conveyor-belt process that builds and then destroys the islands. Together, volcanism and erosion have

Though the landscape appears barren, life is teeming in the rocks and crevices along the trail. Seeds, small plants and insects can be found upon close inspection even a foot off the beaten path. Staying on the trail at all times helps to protect these tiny lives and prevents erosion.
Photo by Peter French

WILLIAM NEIL / LARRY ULRICH

***The most recent lava flow in** the summit area of Haleakalā is about 870 years old. What appears to flow darkly down slope is actually solid rock.*

created a foundation for life in the middle of the wide Pacific Ocean.

One of the basic concepts underlying the creation process of the Hawaiian archipelago is the plate tectonic theory. This theory explains how the surface of the earth is made up of more than a dozen relatively thin, rigid plates that cover the earth like the cracked shell of an egg and "float" on the mantle, a more-or-less fluid layer of super-heated rock. Scientists theorize that thermal convection within the mantle causes these plates to remain in slow but constant motion all over the surface of the earth.

The Pacific plate, on which the islands of Hawai'i are situated, is moving northwesterly toward Japan at the rate of 3-5 inches (7-13 cm) each year. Located in the middle of the Pacific plate, the Hawaiian Islands were formed as the result of the movement of the plate over a hot spot in the earth's mantle. Lava welling out upon the ocean floor for millions of years gradually built the islands one by one, a process that is still going on.

The Hawaiian Islands, then, are actually the very peaks of a long underwater mountain range that is permanently anchored to the continuously moving Pacific plate. Haleakalā itself rises to a height of 10,023 feet (3,055 m) above the surface of the ocean. Below the ocean the mountain descends for another 19,000 feet (5,791 m) to the ocean floor—making it one of the largest mountains on earth when measured from its base. Haleakalā and all the Hawaiian Islands are shield volcanoes, known for their massive broad dome shapes. Formed gradually over thousands of eruptions which add layer upon layer of bulk to the volcano, shield volcanoes are known for their spectacular lava flows and are not generally violently eruptive.

Maui, the second youngest island, still not completely out of the influence of the hot spot, has nevertheless started on an erosional journey that will end only when the island is returned to the sea from which it emerged. The slopes of Maui still appear relatively youthful, but they will one day—like on Kaua'i, its older neighbor to the northwest—bear deep canyons of old age.

Cinders and ʻaʻā lava mix in the foreground and fade to the muted tones of stately cinder cones marching to the summit. The Sliding Sands trail winds faintly in the distance to the Haleakalā Visitor Center perched on the rim, at least a day's hike away. Far from the island's crowded shores, the backcountry of Haleakalā provides the rare experience of being where the ocean is out of sight. Hikers must prepare for this adventure though, as altitude and trails without shade can quickly sap one's energy. Many quarts of water, food, sunscreen, and layers of clothes are required for every trip down the trail.

BOB BUTTERFIELD

BUILDING HALEAKALĀ

The geologic history of Haleakalā above water is estimated to have begun about a million or so years ago, around the time that the woolly mammoth and the saber-toothed tiger roamed the face of the earth. But, the birth of Haleakalā began deep on the ocean floor. Tremendous pressures at these great depths and the relatively low volumes of gas contained in the magma (molten rock) caused the lava flows to form thin, wide-spreading layers. Gradually the mountain neared the surface and the character of the eruption changed. No longer under the weight of thousands of feet of water, red hot lava came into contact with both water and air and caused giant explosions of steam, rock and ash. Billowing, ash-laden clouds, towering thousands of feet into the air, proclaimed the presence of a new volcano and a new island in the Hawaiian chain.

"The slopes of Maui still appear relatively youthful, but they will one day—bear deep canyons of old age."

-11-

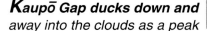

Kaupō Gap ducks down and
*away into the clouds as a peak
called Haleakalā stands sentinel. Adventurous
hikers begin their hike from the summit to the
coast through Kaupō Gap in a matter of days.
The hike traverses nearly each life zone on
the island and is not for the weak-kneed. The
Kaupō trail begins at Palikū and decends
depending on one's beginning point) 6,100 ft.
in just 8.4 miles (1,859m in 13.5km).*

Once the volcanic peak was safely out of the
reach of the waves, lava continued to pour downs-
lope from vents along its rift zones, and the mountain grew steadily toward the sky. It wasn't until the
summit of Haleakalā was several thousand feet
above sea level that its repeated outpourings of lava
washed up against the nearby, much older, volcano
of West Maui, forming the isthmus connecting the
two volcanic peaks of Maui. Since that time, surface
runoff has washed additional material down from

BOB BUTTERFIELD

As wind and
*weather erode
cooled lava, trade
winds mix in soils
and moisture
carried from afar
on the currents.
Then the rocky
ground becomes
a fertile place for rare
plants like ʻiliahi
(sandalwood) and
pilo to grow.*

both mountains to spread a rich layer of alluvium over the older lava flows. The isthmus today is about 7 miles (11 km) across and gives Maui its nickname, "The Valley Isle."

At the end of its shield-building stage, the summit of Haleakalā may have reached a height of 14,500 feet (4,422 m), greater than the current height of Mauna Loa on the island of Hawai'i. The top of that shield eroded away. The old flows underneath were reburied by new eruptions along several rift zones, during the second building stage of Haleakalā.

Three rift zones have been identified running from the summit of Haleakalā: one towards the north, the second to the east, and a third to the southwest. Lava may have issued from vents along any one, two, or all three rift zones at the same time. Practically the entire present summit of Haleakalā is comprised of lava from these eruptions. They form a dense, relatively continuous sheet of lava that is 2,000 feet (600 m) thick near the summit. Soil formations between the layers of lava indicate that the volcano was sometimes quiet for long periods of time between eruptions.

During these quiet periods, the forces of erosion battled the forces of volcanism. Valleys cut by stream erosion were often refilled by lava pouring down the newly cut stream channels. Ultimately, it was erosion that won, carving out the spectacular "crater" of Haleakalā.

Torrential rains brought by prevailing northeast trade winds cut deeper into the north-facing Ke'anae Valley, and to a lesser extent into the Kaupō Valley. These two major gorges were formed with

amphitheater-shaped heads and narrow stream channels. This formation captured many small streams and accelerated the rate and scope of erosion. Waterfalls developed as the valleys carved their way toward the summit and the cascading streams accelerated the carving process.

The large 19-square-mile (49 sq km) summit "crater" was formed not by a summit collapse or by the summit being "blown off" as is often assumed. It is the result of the Ke'anae and Kaupō valleys finally merging to produce a vast depression. Though commonly called a "crater," the striking formation at the summit of Haleakalā is actually more of a valley—7.5 miles (12 km) across and 2.5 miles (4 km) wide—formed by erosional processes. The unique shape of the summit valley was likely established when the two erosional valleys did not meet at the exact summit but were offset to one side of each other. With Ko'olau Gap (leading into Ke'anae Valley) to the north and Kaupō Gap to the south, the "crater" of Haleakalā looks more like a large elbow than the classic circular crater shape.

The erosional process has not stopped. A similar escarpment separates the summit valley from Kīpahulu Valley, with frequent and beautiful waterfalls at Palikū attesting to the constant erosional presence. Someday this valley wall will erode through, forming yet another gap and eventually lengthening the floor of the summit valley.

The colorful cinder cones seen scattered throughout the valley floor were formed during the

Shallow root systems help native plants like na'ena'e to absorb water in the dry summit area. The roots of this fragrant plant were used by Hawaiians to perfume kapa (bark cloth).

__K__uiki peak (7,553 ft, 2,302 m) is the highest point of the ridge that separates the backcountry of Haleakalā with the rainforest of Kīpahulu Valley. The ridgeline catches clouds on both sides dropping 100 inches (254 cm) of rain on Palikū and 400 inches (1,016 cm) in Kīpahulu Valley. More than beautiful, the occasional waterfalls, which may be seen from Palikū, carve deep V-shaped valleys into the ridge, wearing it slowly away.

last major activity phase of Haleakalā, within the last 3,000 years. From explosive (and likely very spectacular) fire fountains along the east rift zone, eruptive material fell back around the vent, forming large cones of cinders. The biggest of all, Pu'u O Māui, is nearly 1,000 feet (300 m) high.

DATING HALEAKALĀ

The most recent chapter in the volcanic history of Haleakalā occurred outside the park along the southwest rift zone in an area known as Honua'ula. There lava from two up-slope vents poured down the flank of the volcano and into the ocean, forming a peninsula and what is now called La Pérouse Bay.

Initially, it was believed that this most recent eruption of Haleakalā occurred in 1790, as determined through oral history and the historic record. Charts created during the voyages of La Pérouse (1786) and Vancouver (1793) were compared, and subtle differences in the description of the same area were found. People questioned in 1841 about the age of the flow stated that their grandparents had observed it, indicating an age of about 1750.

However, in 1999, geologists from the Hawaiian Volcano Observatory obtained radiocarbon dates from these flows that indicate the flows may have occurred as early as 1480. The discrepancy was found while comparing the Haleakalā samples with flows on the island of Hawai'i known to have erupted in 1802. Very different magnetic alignments of the minerals in the two samples were discovered. The Haleakalā samples were actually more similar to flows on Hawai'i dated from 350 to 460 years ago. For now, scientists estimate that the age of the La Pérouse flow is between 220 and 520 years ago, or between the years 1480 and 1780.

Looking upslope from La Pérouse Bay, one sees the site of the most recent eruption of Haleakalā, far from the alpine summit. This cinder cone near the shore erupted between 220-520 years ago. Hawaiian oral histories and maps from early explorers gave the first dates for this flow, which have been recently re-estimated using modern geologic dating techniques.

S. RINGSVEN

"...lava from two up-slope vents poured down the flank of the volcano and into the ocean..."

Geologic dating is an ever-adapting science. New advances in dating technology, as well as oral history accounts, may eventually shed more light on this piece of volcanic history. (Because of its rich archeological resources and its geologic significance as the most recent eruption site of Haleakalā, a Congressional bill was introduced in 2001 proposing a study of the feasibility of adding this area to the national park system.)

With a date of only a few centuries ago, the La Pérouse eruption is very recent in geologic time. This history, and geologic evidence of activity far below the ocean floor in the magma chamber of Haleakalā, indicates that there may be more Haleakalā eruptions yet to come. Therefore, Haleakalā is considered an active, but currently not erupting, volcano. In fact, the final eruption of Haleakalā could occur within our lifetime!

SUGGESTED READING

HAWAIIAN VOLCANO OBSERVATORY. "*Youngest Lava Flows on East Maui Probably Older than AD 1790.*" Volcano Watch. U.S. Geological Survey. Sept. 1999.

HAWAIIAN VOLCANO OBSERVATORY. "*How High Was Haleakalā*" Volcano Watch. U.S. Geological Survey. Feb. 2000.

HAWAIIAN VOLCANO OBSERVATORY. "*Monitoring Kilauea and Mauna Loa with the GPS*" Volcano Watch. U.S. Geological Survey. June 2001.

"O piha, o pihapiha
O piha-u, o piha-a
O lewa ke au
Fruitful, very fruitful
Spreading here, spreading there
The time passes"

-- FROM THE KUMULIPO, HAWAIIAN CREATION CHANT

Wind, Waves and Wings

The Hawaiian Islands are the most isolated island group on the planet. Located in the middle of the Pacific plate, over two thousand miles lie between these islands and the nearest continental land mass. Engulfed by ocean, the high Hawaiian volcanoes make their own weather.

WEATHER-MAKERS AND LIFE ZONES

Ascending the slopes of Haleakalā, the temperature drops about three degrees Fahrenheit per 1,000 feet (one degree Celsius per 174 meters) in elevation. However, between 5,000 and 7,000 feet (1,500 and 2,000 m), there is often a temperature-inversion layer. The inversion forms when heat rises from the surrounding landmass, cools, and creates a "lid" that traps the warm, moist air below. When the prevailing northeast trade winds, heavy with moisture, come into contact with the high-elevation cool air, clouds or rain develop. Rainfall in the Kīpahulu Valley along the northeast (or windward) slope of Haleakalā can reach up to 400 inches (1,016 cm) annually. The inversion layer is responsible for the wreath of clouds that often gently hugs the middle slopes of Haleakalā though clear skies prevail above and below.

While Haleakalā creates its own weather, the weather patterns create the volcano's ecosystems. On Haleakalā, very little moisture falls above the inversion layer. Consequently, vegetation gets more sparse as one travels between 7,000 feet (2,000 m) and the summit at 10,023 feet (3,055 m). At the summit, the landscape seems almost barren with a few hardy plant species surviving on 35 inches (89 cm) or less of precipitation each year. The climatic conditions found at various elevations support an incredible diversity of ecosystems. In fact, while

BRAD LEWIS

New fronds of the 'ama'u (small tree fern) are bright red and age to green as the plant matures. This fern was used as a source of red dye for kapa. During times of famine, ferns became an important food source. Young shoots were eaten raw or cooked and provided a starchy element to the diet.

Nēnē fly again over Haleakalā where they were once extinct. The Hawai'i state bird, nēnē disappeared from Maui due to a combination of habitat loss and predation by alien animals like mongoose. In the early 1960s, a group of Boy Scouts carried nēnē in wooden crates strapped to their backs into the backcounty and helped reintroduce this endangered bird to Haleakalā.

ERIC NISHIBAYASHI

traveling from the Kahului Airport to the summit of Haleakalā—a driving distance of only 37 miles (76km)—one passes through the rough equivalency of life zones encountered by driving north from the latitude of central Mexico to Alaska!

The ecosystems, or life zones, of Haleakalā include alpine/aeolian, subalpine shrubland, rain forest, cloud forest and mesic forest, dry forest and a lowland/coastal zone. Each life zone supports life forms found nowhere else in the world. How life came to be established in this most remote island chain can be seen through the lens of isoltion.

WIND, WAVES AND WINGS

The isolation of the Hawaiian Islands from the rest of the world proved to be both an inhibitor to colonization by plants and animals, and the very thing that caused them to become unique. Plants and animals had to survive the accidental vast trans-oceanic journey to reach these islands. This was no simple matter. Biologists estimate that a single new species successfully colonized the islands on an average of only one every 35,000 years! How was this done? Through the tenacity of seeds and certain animals to travel by wind, waves and on the wings to Hawai'i.

Plants whose seeds can be transported by wind are the best candidates for dispersal to an island. Consequently ferns, whose spores are extremely light, are well represented in Hawai'i with 168 native species. Large plants too can have light seeds. The seeds of the 'ōhi'a tree can drift on winds of less than six miles (10 km) per hour.

Plants favored by birds are also good prospects for long-distance dispersal. Many plant seeds, eaten and retained in digestive tracts of birds or attached externally to their feathers or feet, have made the long journey to the islands. The Pacific golden plover, a migratory shorebird that winters in Hawai'i, may well be responsible for the introduction of plants that occur both in the plover's arctic

The wiliwili, with its distinctive twisted, coral-colored trunk, is endemic to Hawaiʻi. One of the rare deciduous Hawaiian plants, it loses its leaves in the dry summer months. The trunk of the wiliwili was favored by Native Hawaiians who fashioned surfboards and floats for outrigger canoes with the lightweight wood.

JACK JEFFREY

BRAD LEWIS

breeding grounds and in the high-elevation grass-lands within Haleakalā National Park. A few introductions were made to the islands by seeds that floated across the vast ocean to reach Hawaiʻi. Though there are not many seeds capable of withstanding the harsh ocean conditions for extended periods, there are two notable exceptions—the *koa* and the *wiliwili*, trees that are both found in the park. Seeds from the ancestors of these two trees may have floated to the shores of Maui from other islands in the chain, or perhaps from Australia or other islands far to the southwest.

The same factors that limited the arrival of plant life were at least as great a hurdle for animal life. Animals unable to make the journey, like amphibians, reptiles, and nearly all mammals, are not naturally found in the islands. Using the standard of arrival by wind, waves, or wings, only two mammals succeeded in making the accidental journey to Hawaiʻi, the monk seal, which swims; and the Hawaiian bat, which flies.

Once animals arrived at the Hawaiian Islands they faced another challenge—adaptation to their

Koa trees can grow up to 70 ft (21 m) tall with a diameter of up to 10 ft (3 m). Koa forests are found in Kaupō Gap and Kīpahulu Valley. The use of koa for traditional canoes is rooted in Native Hawaiian culture.

-18-

The kōlea (Pacific golden-plover) spends its winters in Hawaiʻi and summers in Alaska. This swift flyer makes the 3,000 mile (4,828 km) non-stop migration in about two days. Kōlea can be found at all elevations from sea level to the summit. The birds arrive in Hawaiʻi appearing thin under their buffy-brown feathers. They feed and fatten up through the fall and winter. Kōlea acquire their breeding plumage in the spring before leaving the islands. Male kōlea then show a dark bottom and gold-speckled back.

JACK JEFFREY

BILL MULL

The Maui cave tree cricket (Thaumatogryllus) is *endemic to lava tubes of East Maui. The cricket, blind, flightless and with pale pigmentation, is well-adapted to a life lived in darkness.*

new environment. Birds met this challenge exceptionally well. Adapting to the environment of Hawaiʻi, and its variety of foods, descendants of a single finch-like ancestor gave rise to an estimated 52 species of native Hawaiian honeycreepers.

It is the insects, however, that show the greatest success in establishment and diversity. From roughly 300 original immigrants, they have expanded into over 7,000 different species, with more being identified each year. In the year 2000, a previously unknown species of blind cave cricket was discovered during road construction near the summit of Haleakalā.

The diversity of life found in Hawaiʻi today is a product of both beating the odds of arrival and adaptation in isolation. Faced with a wide variety of fresh habitats, the successful colonizers adapted in different ways to the new environment. Through the process of adaptive radiation, these species differentiated enough to become almost unrecognizable when compared with their ancestors.

Biologists continue to study Hawaiian species as textbook products of evolutionary processes. The great diversity found within a species occurring at sea level and on mountain tops and forests led early scientists to erroneously believe they had discovered many more species than they truely found. Further study revealed that some of the supposedly new species were actually the many different forms of only one species. Some of the plant types adapted their leaf size, overall shape, or degree of hairiness to cope with the different environmental conditions found in the vertical geography of the islands. Thus the *pūkiawe* and the *'ōhi'a* growing in dry-forest conditions vary considerably from those of the same species found in rain forest habitats.

The absence of large grazing animals and predators—because of their natural inability to cross the ocean barrier—has significantly influ-

***T**he absence of large herbivores caused many* native Hawaiian plants to evolve without thorns, noxious chemicals, or bad tastes—like the Hawaiian "mintless" mint.

Nēnē feed on berries in the backcountry, not the most suitable habitat for a goose. Yet, Haleakalā National Park provides protection from predators, allowing nēnē a chance for survival. The nēnē population in the park is relatively static between 200-250 birds. Goslings have a low survival rate and park biologists are trying to determine the cause. Low sources of nutrition may be a factor. Another may be loss. Nēnē mate for life and if a partner dies or is killed, it may take several productive years before a new mate is chosen.

The sharp eyes of the native pueo
(Hawaiian owl) watch for prey. Pueo are often
seen soaring over summit slopes in late
afternoon.

JACK JEFFREY

JACK JEFFREY

The long orange beak
of the ʻiʻiwi is a perfect
fit to sip nectar from a māmane tree.

enced the development of island flora and fauna. No longer required to ensure their survival through protective measures, almost all of the plants of Hawaiʻi are without thorns, offensive odors, and toxic substances. The thornless ʻākala (raspberry) and odorless mint are but two examples in Haleakalā.

Mutations among some Hawaiian birds resulted in flightlessness. Flight was not a critical need in an environment where there were no ground-dwelling animal predators. At least four species of flightless geese (known through their fossil remains) shared pre-historic Maui with the nēnē (Hawaiian goose). With the arrival of efficient land-based predators, in the form of people and the mammals they introduced to the islands, the flightless adaptation became a liability to survival. Of the large ground dwellers, only the nēnē, a capable flier, remains.

The most recent major introductions to Hawaiian ecosystems have been brought by the new kinds of mechanical wind, wave and wing powers in this modern world of frequent and far-reaching travel. Disease, predators and invasive plant species are regularly introduced (either purposely or accidentally) to Hawaiʻi. Whereas it once required thousands of years for a single species to successfully colonize in Hawaiʻi, today about 20 alien species are established in Hawaiʻi every year. Over the years since the arrival of people, the unique biology of native flora and fauna has often succumbed to the human desire for a controlled environment. With most of the coastal areas developed today, the volcanic mountain tops are among the last homes for native species.

Thus, the primary reason for the existence of Haleakalā National Park is clear—to preserve resources which are linked together in a critical web of life. From its volcanic birth to today, Haleakalā supports a diversity of life zones that in turn provide the last (and in some cases the only) home for many Hawaiian plant and animal species.

SUGGESTED READING

HAWAIʻI AUDUBON SOCIETY. *Hawaiʻi's Birds*. Honolulu: Hawaiʻi Audubon Society, 1997 (reprint).

HOWARTH, FRANCIS G. AND WILLIAM P. MULL. *Hawaiian Insects and Their Kin*. Honolulu: University of Hawaiʻi Press, 1992.

MEDEIROS, ARTHUR AND LLOYD LOOPE. *Rare Animals and Plants of Haleakalā National Park*. Hawaiʻi Natural History Association, 1994.

S. RINGSVEN

The characteristic stalk of the ʻāhinahina (Haleakalā silversword) signals the one and only bloom in the plant's life. Up to five hundred purplish flowers open progressively from bottom to top in about two weeks time. The pungent honey-sweet scent of a blooming ʻāhinahina attracts native insect pollinators and delighted visitors alike to witness this final show. After blooming, the ʻāhinahina sets its seeds to the wind and dies.

JACK JEFFREY

JACK JEFFREY

The greensword is a close relative of the silversword and shares many of the growing habits of its cousin. Greenswords are found in open bogs and rain forests where the annual rainfall averages several hundred inches. In variation from the silversword, greenswords lack the protective silvery hairs on their leaves because they grow in a much wetter environment. These plants are often branched and look shrubby. Even in their remote location, greenswords have been subjected to predation by feral pigs and goats. Where fenced exclosures have kept non-native grazing animals out, these and other native plants have recovered dramatically. This focus on protection allows scientists to continue to document and observe the rare plants found in the bogs of Haleakalā.

DAVID MUENCH

The silversword has become so entwined with popular knowledge of Haleakalā that generations have traveled to the summit just to see it. Visitors occasionally removed plants for lei or parade float decorations, proof of their trip to Haleakalā. Today's park visitors protect this threatened species by taking only pictures of the rare plant.

Overleaf: Looking toward Kaupō Gap to the southern shore of Haleakalā, one understands that there is more to this mountain than first meets the eye. Photo by David Muench.

"Nani ke ao i Haleakalā
'Ohu'ohu i ka noe o uka
Beautiful are the clouds of Haleakalā
Adorned with the mists of the upland"

--FROM NANI KE AO I HALEAKALĀ

A Slice of "Old Hawai'i"

BOB BUTTERFIELD

Kīpahulu, on the eastern shore of Maui, is a tropical paradise unlike any other. This area provides the coastal contrast to the park's cindery summit area. The Kīpahulu district showcases one of the richest botanical regions in Hawai'i, from high-elevation bogs and grasslands to forests of native *koa* and *'ōhi'a* to a thick mixture of native and alien plants that spill towards rugged sea cliffs. The remoteness of this part of Maui, still experienced by today's visitors during the twisty drive along the Hāna Highway, has allowed the plants, animals and people of Kīpahulu to live in relative isolation for centuries. Here is a place with the feeling of "Old Hawai'i," a feeling that is carried into the 21st century by the success of a very old concept—*mālama 'aina* (taking care of the land).

Mālama 'aina is the concept of land conservation that Hawaiians have used for generations to provide for the preservation of natural resources, thereby sustaining the human life inherently connected to those resources. The idea of using only what is needed and preserving the rest for the future has been passed down through multiple generations and is still practiced in the everyday life of modern Hawaiians. *Mālama 'aina* was further sup-

Beauty on both sides, Highway 31 passes through the edge of one of Haleakalā National Park's newest sections—Ka'apahu. Visitors often stop to enjoy the view as fresh water mingles with the sea at the mouths of 'Ālelele and Lelekea Streams. Added to the park in 1999, this spectacular area joins with Kīpahulu Valley to protect rare natural and cultural resources.

JACK JEFFREY

Representing gods in earthly form, used to create tools and canoes, its blossoms strung in lei of old and of today, the 'Ōhi'a lehua is both respected and honored. 'Ōhi'a are one of the predominant native tree species in the lush forests of windward Haleakalā. In the park's Kīpahulu Valley Biological Reserve, ancient stands are intact and protected for the future.

ported in old times by a land division system unique to this island culture.

Land was divided in triangle-shaped sections originating from a narrow point at the summit of the volcano and expanding to broader areas near the sea. These *moku* or districts circled the island and provided all the people living within the *moku* with the stuff of life—natural resources from the mountain forests to the fertile sea.

These districts were further sub-divided into several *ahupua'a*, smaller sections of land stretching from the mountain to the sea in which family groups lived and worked. The eight ancient *moku* of East Maui radiate from a central point near Haleakalā Crater called *Pōhaku Palaha*. Kīpahulu is one of these ancient districts, containing several *ahupua'a*, whose boundaries are said to have been established about twenty generations back.

Archeological evidence shows us that Kīpahulu once supported an extensive community of farmers, fishermen, bird-catchers, canoe-makers and their families. Numerous pre-contact (prior to 1778) Hawaiian structures, including habitation sites, *lo'i* (taro patches), and *heiau* (places of worship/shrines) can still be seen in the landscape.

Many *ali'i* from the island of Hawai'i made their home at Kīpahulu. Battles between these chiefs were fought to gain control of the desirable Kīpahulu and Hāna districts. Two were fought near Lelekea in the Ka'apahu area to the south of Kīpahulu, a recent addition to Haleakalā National Park. The Lelekea valley divides the Kīpahulu and Kaupō districts. One translation of Lelekea—"breath flown"—is said to have come from the occasion of ancient *ail'i* being brought to Ka'apahu for rest and healing, yet ultimately passing away there.

North of Kīpahulu in the district of Hāna, Queen Ka'ahumanu, the favorite wife of King Kamehameha I, was born. It was also at Hāna that

NPS PHOTO

Pi'ilanihale Heiau is the largest heiau in the Hawaiian Islands. Heiau are places of worship constructed by Hawaiians hundreds of years ago. Heiau were built to honor the sacredness of specific places or activities (like fishing). Some heiau were elaborately constructed, others are small simple shrines. Pi'ilanihale Heiau is a massive stone platform built atop a natural lava hill. It is in Kahanu Garden near the town of Hāna, and has been recently restored. Privately owned outside of the park, the heiau is listed on the National Register of Historic Places. Public tours of the grounds are offered.

Chief 'Umi a Liloa, of the island of Hawai'i, defeated the forces of Maui and claimed it as a territory of his home island. Through a long and bitter struggle, Chief Kahekili, of Maui, recaptured Hāna by cutting off the water supply to the invader's fortress on Ka'uiki, the large hill beside Hāna Bay. So it was water that won the battle, and water that provided life to the people of the *moku*.

WATER FOR LIFE

Water, especially fresh water, is a critical force in sustaining life on this planet. It is a precious commodity in an island chain in a salt-water world. Kīpahulu valley, rising up to over 7,300 feet (2,227 m), becomes a natural "rain-catcher" for the moisture heavy northeast trade winds.

Rain falling at the higher elevations, nearly 400 inches (1,016 cm) a year, makes its way down the valley through a series of streams, the longest of which is Palikea. Beginning in upper Kīpahulu Valley, Palikea Stream, at 10 miles (16 km) in length, is the longest stream on Maui. With its tributary, the

Pīpīwai Stream, the Palikea rushes over several waterfalls and plunges through dozens of natural pools before traveling its last land mile through 'Ohe'o Gulch and emptying into the ocean.

In ancient times, this stream, and its surrounding natural springs and tributaries, fed hundreds of people in the Kīpahulu District by providing an ideal climate for agriculture. Flowing into the lower elevations, the water nourished multiple patches of taro, a starchy plant that is a staple of the Hawaiian diet and culturally tied to the origin of the Hawaiian people.

Plants like bananas, sweet potatoes and taro (brought to the islands by early Hawaiians) complimented the supply of fish caught in the ocean below. Freshwater native 'o'opu (fish) and 'ōpae (shrimp) were caught in Palikea Stream and can still be found there today by the careful observer.

Within one area of ancient *lo'i* on the banks of the Palikea, taro, bananas, sweet potatoes and sugarcane are once again back in production. Through agreements with local Native Hawaiians, Haleakalā

-28-

National Park supports the cultivation of traditional agricultural plants in patches brought back to life. Over 2.5 acres (1 hectare) of *lo'i* are green again and producing taro that is shared at community gatherings and festivals. Farming traditions are passed on to *na keiki* (children) who work in the rich mud. This partnership also provides for public tours where visitors learn about farming and the cultural significance of *taro* from Hawaiians whose families have been tied to this area for generations.

To help preserve the vital watershed of East Maui, Haleakalā National Park has entered into partnership with neighboring private and state landholders. The East Maui Watershed Partnership cooperates to monitor natural resources of a watershed that spreads for over 100,000 acres (40,500 hectares). Each agency contributes to the fight to maintain the health of this watershed by controlling invasive alien plants like miconia and building fences to control feral animal populations that root out native plants. Together, they hope to ensure the long-term survival of the East Maui watershed—native ecosystems that are the home to hundreds of threatened and endangered species as well as thousands of people who now live in East Maui.

PROTECTING KĪPAHULU

The push to preserve Kīpahulu began in 1951 when Congress authorized the acquisition of nearly 9,000 acres (3,645 hectares) of land in the upper Kīpahulu Valley for addition to Haleakalā National Park. At the time, not many details were known about the specific resources found in Kīpahulu Valley. The Nature Conservancy sponsored a scientific expedition throughout the length of the valley in 1967. It was then that the world became aware of the incredible rarity and diversity of plant life found within the valley. Dr. Charles Lamoureux, one of the expedition scientists, reported:

"Within three miles one can find communities ranging from a tropical rain forest to a subalpine zone with frequent frosts. Elsewhere in Hawai'i today it would be nearly impossible to find this many undisturbed communities in such close proximity. Since most of the Hawaiian species of plants are endemic, these communities are like no others, and Kīpahulu in this sense offers an opportunity not available elsewhere on this planet."

The Nature Conservancy raised money to acquire the privately owned lands within the Kīpahulu Valley to donate to the National Park if

Ancient lo'i (taro patches) brought back to life provide a snapshot of a time when traditional agriculture covered the mid-elevation slopes of Haleakalā. Water trickles through the terraced patches of Kapahu Farm giving life to this staple crop and cultural symbol. Farming of the lo'i is done through a partnership with Native Hawaiians who trace their ancestors to these same Kīpahulu fields.

BOB BUTTERFIELD

the State of Hawai'i would agree to donate its land within the valley to the federal government as well. Local landowners in the lower valley discussed the possibility of making their joint land a park. Laurance Rockefeller supported the effort by purchasing 52 acres of lower Kīpahulu, including the 'Ohe'o area, from local landowners to in turn donate to Haleakalā National Park.

Rockefeller and The Nature Conservancy formally donated the lands to the National Park Service in 1969. The state donated its lands in 1974, thereby completing over two decades of effort to preserve the outstanding scenic and scientific resources of Kīpahulu for the future. These resources, traditionally protected by the Native Hawaiian practice of *mālama 'āina*, would now also be conserved by a parallel concept—the mission of the National Park Service.

A VALLEY OF REFUGE FOR ENDANGERED SPECIES

Before modern scientific explorations documented the rare and endangered species of the upper Kīpahulu Valley, humans had rarely set foot in this nearly impenetrable place. Early Hawaiians considered the high valley *kapu* (taboo/forbidden). In old Hawaiian society, the higher a person was in rank, the closer that *ali'i* (chief) was to the gods. Similarly, lands of the higher elevations were closer to the gods and thus left to the *ali'i*. Common people used the resources found in the lower elevation forests and made their homes near the coast. The long-term lack of human contact allowed the native plants and animals of the upper valley to flourish, developing into unique species found nowhere else in the world. The variety of these endemic species has been called "unparralleled."

Botanical studies have indicated that the plant community of the forest is about ninety percent native. It contains at least four rare native birds, including the Maui *nukupu'u*, previously thought to be extinct. Park scientists have found several individual plants which may turn out to be a new species of the endemic genus Cyanea. Once these plants mature and flower, park botanists will determine if they are of a species that has not been collected in many years, or if they represent a new species that has been discovered in this protected valley.

High in Kīpahulu Valley, water cascades down one of many waterfalls. The plunging stream forms a series of natural pools that feed a diverse mix of life in this rain forest.

A typical view in the Kīpahulu Valley Biological Reserve, the lush mix of vegetation provides a glimpse of what ancient Hawaiian rainforests may have looked like. Years after Kīpahulu Valley was added to the park, scientists are still inventorying the valley, and still discovering new species. The biota of Kīpahulu Valley is unique and fragile and remains the best surviving example of a native Hawaiian rainforest.

BOB BUTTERFIELD

BOB BUTTERFIELD

*P*ark botanists propagate native plants from seeds and cuttings in the remote rainforest. To aid in re-establishing native species to an area, young individuals are planted after the removal of alien vegetation. Botanists wear slickers and hats for comfort and plastic gloves to protect them from rooting hormones while working in the rainforest nurseries.

I In order to continue the natural preservation of these resources, then, National Park Service Director George Hartzog announced during his acceptance of the Kīpahulu lands that, "use of the Kīpahulu Valley acreage will be limited to the valley's lower reaches. The nearly inaccessible upper slopes are to be preserved in a natural state for scientific purposes."

The area was designated the Kīpahulu Valley Biological Reserve, a key refuge for endangered Hawaiian plant and animal species. The Biological Reserve does not have any trails and is closed to the public. Like the Hawaiian *kapu* on entry to this area, Haleakalā National Park has ensured that the last remaining example of a pristine Hawaiian rain forest will not be drastically altered by the developments of humankind.

SUGGESTED READING

NATIONAL PARK SERVICE. *General Management Plan/ Environmental Impact Statement*. Haleakalā National Park, 1995.

SELLARS, RICHARD WEST. *Preserving Nature in the National Parks*. New Haven: Yale University Press, 1997.

STERLING, ELSPETH P. *Sites of Maui*. Honolulu: Bishop Museum Press, 1998.

Rare, Endangered, Endemic

All native plant and animal life in Hawai'i is rare because of its relative isolation from the rest of the world. Some species are more rare than others. Haleakalā is home to over 180 endemic Hawaiian plants; over 40 of those are endemic to Maui. Endemic species are highly adapted to their local environment and cannot be found anywhere else. Haleakalā is also home to numerous threatened and endangered species. Some species are endangered from the moment they are discovered. The introduction of alien plants and animals disrupts the balance of native ecosystems, bringing a very real threat of extinction to native species. By continuing to protect and restore critical habitat in places like Haleakalā, humans help perpetuate the mosaic of native life found only in Hawai'i.

JACK JEFFREY

The 'akohekohe (crested honeycreeper), is found only on East Maui. It is one of more than 50 species of native Hawaiian honeycreepers that evolved from a single original species.

Native species of Hawaiian geranium are called nohoanu. Their silvery leaves reflect light, even moonlight, giving them a second name, hinahina.

BOB BUTTERFIELD

JACK JEFFREY

The native common mint (Stenogyne kamehamehae) trails along the ground of wet Hawaiian rain forests.

The budding leaves of the 'ōhi'a form a beautiful cluster of new life.

BOB BUTTERFIELD

This rare species of nohoanu only grows as a shrub and is found in lower alpine areas of Haleakalā.

JACK JEFFREY

The native *lobelioids* of Hawai'i represent one of the best examples of co-evolution anywhere. The long, curved floral tubes of the lobelia are a perfect fit for the curved beaks of native honeycreepers.

Many plants of the genus Peperomia are epiphytic, gaining support, but no nutrients, by growing on other plants.

The remote montane bogs of Haleakalā host a variety of rare plants, like the greensword. These bogs are between 5,300-7,400 feet (1,615-2,256 m) elevation and were virtually unknown until the 1970's.

Astelia bug
(Asteliamiris johpolhemi)

Flightless moth
(Thyrocopa apatela)

Discovered only in Kīpahulu Valley, the "Astelia bug" was so different from its other relatives that a new genus and species were created to classify it in 1999. This tiny insect feeds on the leaves of the Astelia plant, instead of on grasses like its cousins. Another endemic insect, found only in the summit area of Haleakalā, is the flightless moth. Carried by the wind, this scavenger feeds on organic debris wherever it lands.

*"**O**h Haleakalā! With thy summits high,*

Far towering towards the eastern sky.

Wherever I may roam, Whate'er realms I may see,

My heart untravelled fond—by turns to thee."

-- AUGUST 24, 1915 ENTRY IN THE HALEAKALĀ
RESTHOUSE LOGBOOK BY A.M. SAONG

Those Who Came Before...

*****P**alikea stream
and the pools of
'Ohe'o still bring
life giving water to
the people of
Kīpahulu. Here
stories of
ancestors are not
dim echoes. The
mana (power) of
the place and the
traditions of the past
reverberate in chants
and conch shell calls by
Hawaiians who sustain
the culture.*

BOB BUTTERFIELD

The human story of Haleakalā begins long after native plants and animals had established themselves on these volcanic shores. The first people to arrive in Hawai'i, Polynesians, crossed three different regions of prevailing winds and ocean currents, sailing north over 2,000 miles (3,218 km) of open ocean in hand-carved canoes to reach this land. Without the aid of a modern-day compass or map, Polynesians navigated using natural signs (such as constellations, cloud formations and sea swells) to guide them. Polynesians reached the Hawaiian Islands from East Polynesia some time before 1200 years ago.

Early Hawaiians gave this island chain the name Havai'i, after the legendary ancestral homeland for the Polynesian people. They called themselves simply *Kānaka Maoli* (the people). Through time, the island of Maui became known for a demigod famous throughout Polynesia. Māui was a strong, clever trickster who, among many feats, "fished" the islands from the sea and snared the sun. The mountain from which Māui snared the sun was called 'Alehelā (snare-sun) or 'Aheleakalā (rays of the sun)…today called Haleakalā (house of the sun).

ERIC NISHIBAYASHI

***W**hen the misty clouds shroud Haleakalā Crater, visitors occasionally witness a rare phenomenon. With one's back to the sun and clouds below, the angle of the afternoon sun may cast a shadow onto the mist, surrounding it in a complete rainbow. The effect is called the Specter of the Brôcken. Seeing a shadow of oneself suspended above the clouds, enclosed in color, may put visitors in mind of those who stood before them on these lofty heights.*

Though Māui is said to have made the trip to the summit of Haleakalā at least once, Hawaiians commonly would not have made the long land voyage from their home at the coast. Only people with a particular task would make the trip.

Bird catchers would venture into the upper elevation forests for the bright red and yellow feathers of native birds for fashioning into chiefly cloaks. The dense basalt near the summit was quarried for adze (stone tools). Religious ceremonies and burials took place at the summit and in its deep cinder-cone studded valley. At least one *heiau* was built on the rim of the summit valley and ancient trails allowed passage up and over the mountain.

Evidence of this activity can still be seen in *pā* (rock enclosures), which were used as temporary shelters, scattered throughout the summit landscape. The summit environment was too cold and provided little food to make permanent habitation possible. Instead, the summit of Haleakalā was essentially a sacred place, visited, but not occupied.

A SEA OF CHANGE

By the time Captain James Cook sailed into view of northeast shore of Maui in November 1779, the native population was estimated at 124,000 people. Though Cook stayed anchored near Maui for several days, he never came ashore.

The first Westerner to come ashore was Admiral La Pérouse in May of 1786. The bay where he landed, the site of the most recent eruption of Haleakalā at Keone'ō'io, was later renamed La Pérouse Bay in his honor.

Soon the adventure and profit of sea exploration captured the rest of the world. Hawai'i became a favorite stopping place in the Pacific, in part because of the diversity of unique, and therefore valuable natural resources. A preference for the fragrant sandalwood tree, especially in Asia, began the lucrative sandalwood trade in the 1790s. 'Iliahi (sandalwood) was harvested from the slopes of Haleakalā to near extinction. Today, only six to eight hundred individuals of the native Haleakalā sandalwood can be found in the upper elevations.

Hala are found in the coastal areas of *Haleakalā, especially Kīpahulu. These trees are easily recognized for their sturdy prop roots, branching out like fingers from the base. The long serrated leaves grow in broad spirals. Lau hala (leaves) from this native tree were used for roof thatching on hale (traditional buildings) and for weaving mats—a practice common today.*

"We beheld the seat of Pele's dreadful reign."

When the sandalwood trade began to die out, New England whalers and missionaries were already floating into Maui harbors. The first written account of a summit ascent of Haleakalā came in the mid 1820s from three missionaries who spent an uncomfortable night on the rugged slopes. Upon their return, they declared:

"We beheld the seat of Pele's dreadful reign. We stood on the edge of a tremendous crater, down which, a single misstep would have precipitated us, 1,000 or 1,500 feet. This was once filled with liquid fire, and in it, we counted sixteen extinguished craters."

In 1841 the summit area was again explored and described, this time by members of the U.S. Exploring Expedition commanded by Charles Wilkes. The expedition map of the inner volcano was the first to be published.

CATTLE, CANE AND TOURISTS

Cattle were first introduced in Hawai'i by George Vancouver in the 18th century. Cattle ranching later became big business and several ranches were established on the slopes of Haleakalā. The Haleakalā Ranch used both the western flanks and the summit of Haleakalā for grazing. Cattle were driven down the Sliding Sands Trail, and later, the Halemau'u Trail, to the lush eastern end of the "crater" at Palikū. From Palikū, ranchers would drive their cattle up to the Kalapawili Ridge (north

Traditional tools are *still used by Hawaiian canoe-builders, poi-makers and fishermen. Adze, poi pounders, pestles and lures are crafted from stone, wood, bone, shell and hand-woven cord.*

of Palikū) where vegetation and a freshwater lake provided pasture for up to three months at a time! Cattle ranching was introduced in Kīpahulu in 1928 and proved to be fairly successful.

While acres of land were cleared of native vegetation to support cattle, acres more were cleared for sugarcane plantations. Polynesians introduced a variety of sugarcane when they arrived in Hawai'i, but the first raw sugar was not produced here until 1802. Interest in sugar grew rapidly in East Maui. A mill at Kīpahulu began production in 1881. Sugar operations in Kīpahulu were not a huge success with the problem of transporting the product over steep slopes and deep gulches. The Kīpahulu sugar mill closed its doors in 1925. The old mill site, privately owned, can be easily seen from the road today on the Kaupō side of the Kīpahulu park lands, about one mile from 'Ohe'o Bridge.

By the early 1900s, sugar and cattle were major exports for Maui, yet each ship brought more visitors. At the turn of the century, an ascent to the summit of Haleakalā was the primary attraction for Maui visitors. However, the trip was long and wearisome. After the windy daylong ascent on horseback to the summit, visitors shivered through the nights in caves. A resthouse near the summit was constructed in 1894. The resthouse, built near the present day Kalahaku Overlook at 9,324 feet (2,842 m), provided a more secure environment to weather the changeable summit conditions and allowed visitors a much more comfortable stay after such a long trip.

Visitors then, as now, continue to be struck by the quiet immensity of Haleakalā. An early guide to the summit of Haleakalā, Worth Aiken, introduced many notable visitors to the summit and trails of the "crater" on horseback. When Aiken brought naturalist John Burroughs to the summit in the late 1920s, he declared it one of the most pleasant experiences of his life. Aiken recalled the moment, summing up what many feel upon seeing Haleakalā Crater.

"When, upon reaching the crater, the view burst upon him, he [Burroughs] stood with bated breath, spellbound for about ten minutes, and then turning slowly to me said, 'Mr. Aiken, I can say in all sincerity that this is the grandest sight of my life.' Later, he wrote me… to stand staunchly by old Haleakalā, for Kilauea is a glimpse into the depths of Hell, but Haleakalā is a view of the glories of Heaven: and were the privilege ever given to me to see again one of the two, I would without hesitation return to Haleakalā."

Native 'ama'u (fern) and 'ōhi'a are protected at Palikū where cattle were once brought to graze.
Prior to cattle, goats had established themselves by the hundreds in the Haleakalā backcountry. Without predators, feral goats ate their way through native forests. The park established a fencing program along its boundaries in 1986 to keep out these non-native herbivores. It works, but the next threat is on the horizon—axis deer, which can easily jump fences.

BOB BUTTERFIELD

Establishing a Hawaiian National Park

With its 1898 annexation, Hawai'i became a territory of the United States. Across the U.S. Mainland, the push to preserve scenic natural lands of inspirational beauty had created the first national parks in the world. Conservationists wanted to expand the system by creating a national park in the territory of Hawai'i. There was also a strong desire to provide comprehensive management of the new national parks through a single federal agency.

The National Park Service was established by Congress on August 25, 1916. Hawai'i National Park was established 24 days earlier on August 1, 1916. Hawai'i National Park consisted of three units: the summit area of Haleakalā on Maui, and portions of Kilauea and Mauna Loa volcanoes on the island of Hawai'i.

Unfortunately, mere designation as a national park was not enough to protect it. In fact, there were congressmen who did not want to give any money to the new park stating: "It should not cost anything to run a volcano." But curious visitors and vandals were pulling up and selling rare silversword plants. Feral pigs and goats were overgrazing the native vegetation and causing serious erosion from their hooves and rooting.

Finally, in 1922, funding was provided for the first Hawai'i National Park personnel. The first superintendent, Thomas Boles, made his headquarters at Kilauea on Hawai'i. He stated that the "crater" of Haleakalā was a wonderful asset to the National Park Service and would become the means for obtaining a large increase in the number of visitors to Hawai'i National Park. However, there needed to be an easier way for visitors to reach the summit.

The Maui parrotbill forages for insects by ripping bark with its massive beak. This bird is endemic and endangered, only an estimated 500 individuals remain.

Visitors may catch a quick glimpse of the yellow-green 'amakihi in the summit area. The Hosmer Grove nature trail provides good opportunities to view native birds.

A Road, a War, and a New Haleakalā

The first focus of the new superintendent was to construct a sufficient road into the park at Haleakalā. The design for the new road was finished by 1933 and construction began. The park road was completed two years later, causing a celebration throughout the island. Local Maui businesses closed and the Territorial Legislature adjourned in order to join the dedication ceremonies along with 1,600 other people. By 1937, ten times that number traveled to the park via the new road.

With a greater number of people visiting the park, and the country in a Great Depression, there came an opportunity to provide both jobs and recreational access at Haleakalā. The Civilian Conservation Corps (CCC) came to the Territory of Hawai'i and established a CCC camp at Haleakalā

by 1934. The crews built and repaired trails, constructed the backcountry cabins, and built water tanks to provide an early, and much needed, source of water for the increasing number of visitors to the dry summit area. These CCC crews became some of the first "official" vegetation crews in the park, removing alien vegetation and clearing firebreaks around the park boundary.

When World War II reached Hawaiian shores on December 7, 1941, the Army was constructing an aircraft warning system at the summit of Haleakalā. Operating staff were stationed at a base camp constructed near the park entrance. Due to the presence of the defense facilities at the summit, the Army ordered the closure of the Haleakalā section of Hawai'i National Park to the public. Haleakalā remained closed for 14 months as the war progressed.

BOB BUTTERFIELD

Enclaves of early development in
the Wilderness Area of Haleakalā,
four historic cabins still provide overnight shelter to those seeking solitude. Built by the Civilian Conservation
Corps in 1937, the cabins are important cultural resources. At Palikū, a visitor cabin and a ranger patrol cabin
blend into the landscape. Visitors must enter a lottery in advance to enjoy enjoy these rustic accommodations.

When the last military personnel left the park in 1946, all of their buildings were transferred to the management of the National Park Service. Several of the buildings, including converted officers quarters and a radio building, became Haleakalā National Park's first and only concession operation in 1947—the Haleakalā Mountain Lodge (later called the Silversword Inn). Instead of coming by horseback and staying in a cave or cement resthouse, visitors could now drive to the lodge, have a warm meal and a cozy bed before traveling the remaining 10 miles (16 km) to the summit. The lodge closed in 1961, no longer needed with the advent of modern roads and ease of travel.

Nearly fifty years after its birth, Hawai'i National Park was redesignated as two new national parks. In 1960, Congress authorized the Haleakalā section of Hawai'i National Park to be, "established as a separate unit of the national park system to be known as Haleakala* National Park." The Hawai'i units became Hawai'i Volcanoes National Park—sister parks forevermore.

SUGGESTED READING

BARTHOLOMEW, GAIL. *Maui Remembers: A Local History*. Honolulu: Mutual Publishing, 1994.

JUVIK, SONIA P. AND JAMES O. JUVIK, editors. *Atlas of Hawai'i*. Third edition. Honolulu, HI: University of Hawai'i Press. 1998.

KĀNE, HERB KAWAINUI. *Ancient Hawai'i*. Captain Cook: The Kawainui Press, 1997.

MAPS:

MAP OF MAUI, *The Valley Isle*. Sixth edition. Honolulu, HI: University of Hawai'i Press. 1997.

HALEAKALĀ NATIONAL PARK, *Hawai'i, Trails Illustrated* Topo Maps. Evergreen, CO: Trails Illustrated, Ponderosa Publishing Company. 1991

Haleakalā, in the original legislation, was written without its appropriate diacritical mark as Haleakala. Public Law 106-510, passed in 2000, added the macron to correctly identify the park's true name, Haleakalā National Park. Diacritical marks are used to help readers properly pronounce Hawaiian words. For example, the use of a kahakō (macron) over the final a in Haleakalā indicates that the final sound is stressed and held a little longer than the other vowels. A simple mispronunciation can drastically change the meaning of a Hawaiian word! Pronounced without the kahakō , Haleakala means "house of the unicorn fish". Pronounced with the kahakō, Haleakalā means "house of the sun" which is the volcano's ancient name.

> *"After an endless, restless night
> someone discovers it is 3:30 a.m.
> and we must be up and off to the summit."*
>
> --WORTH AIKEN, HALEAKALĀ GUIDE, 1891-1935

Being at Haleakalā

BRAD LEWIS

Bold and broad, the expanse and detail of Haleakalā Crater thrill first-time visitors to the summit. In Kīpahulu, the ocean stretches to the horizon and the mountain fills the sky. A visit to Haleakalā National Park can surprise and inspire, awe and calm. More than just a drive to the summit or the coast, a closer look reveals connections between plants and birds, people and water, the land and life.

Here you can experience first-hand the results of volcanism and erosion, processes that are both unique and ongoing. You can ramble through a rain forest, lush and green, warm and wet. Let your feet take a hike into a remote volcanic wilderness where silence reigns and only the wind disturbs the air. Come at night so your eyes may study the sky and find the star that drew the first Polynesians to these islands. Those who take the time to pause find that Haleakalā has imprinted a piece of itself on their mind and heart, an experience they never forget.

On a clear day, hikers on the Halemau'u Trail get a fantastic view of both the backcountry and *Ko'olau Gap*. The *Halemau'u Trail* is known for its "switchbacks" leading from the valley floor to the trailhead over 1000 ft (304 m) above. It is one of two main trails that provide access to the backcountry from the summit area.

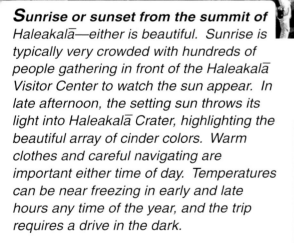

BRAD LEWIS

***Sunrise* or *sunset* from the summit of** *Haleakalā—either is beautiful. Sunrise is typically very crowded with hundreds of people gathering in front of the Haleakalā Visitor Center to watch the sun appear. In late afternoon, the setting sun throws its light into Haleakalā Crater, highlighting the beautiful array of cinder colors. Warm clothes and careful navigating are important either time of day. Temperatures can be near freezing in early and late hours any time of the year, and the trip requires a drive in the dark.*

BRAD LEWIS

***Leave No Trace* ethics are** *important in both the backcountry and developed areas. Stay on the trail to protect fragile plants and insects. Pack it in, pack it out. Take pictures and leave the resources intact for the next visitor to enjoy.*

Many explore Haleakalā on horseback, either on a commercial ride or with their own stock. Some local families have been enjoying a bit of wilderness this way for generations. There are over 24,000 acres (9,712 hectares) of designated wilderness in the park.

BOB BUTTERFIELD

A night at Kapalaoa cabin puts hikers at least 3 miles (4 km) from anyone else. Here one finds silence, broken only by the honks of *nēnē* (Hawaiian goose) during the day and the haunting cries of *'ua'u* (dark-rumped petrel) at night.

BRAD LEWIS

BRAD LEWIS

Bicyclists must share the road with cars and busses on their trip down the mountain. Dressed in rain suits and helmets, hundreds of cyclists make the descent from the summit with commercial tour companies every day.

BRAD LEWIS

BRAD LEWIS

Designated campsites allow visitors to enjoy the backcountry without being crowded. Backcountry camping requires a wilderness camping permit.

Horses are allowed overnight at Hōlua and Palikū. Park staff also use horses and mules as transportation in order to maintain the backcountry cabins. Remember to give horses the right-of-way on the trail. Quietly stand to one side and do not make quick movements that may startle the animals.

The pools of ‘Ohe‘o in Kīpahulu are beautiful and provide many forms of refreshment. Hawaiians traditionally fished in these pools and today's visitors often pause for a quick dip. Flash flooding in this mountain-fed stream can occur rapidly, even when there are clear skies overhead. Visitors swim at their own risk and should be mindful of posted signs or rising water.

PETER FRENCH

The 'ahinahina (Haleakalā silversword) tells a story of survival in the summit area of Haleakalā. Found only between 7,000-10,023 ft (2,134-3,055 m) on Haleakalā, this species of silversword is well adapted to the dry, rocky ecosystem. Living for ages without predators, silversword populations dramatically declined after goats were introduced to the area. The soft silvery leaves were no defense against the hungry mouths and sharp hooves of goats. Active feral animal management and the park's fencing program have eliminated ranging goats from Haleakalā and the silversword is on the rebound. Now young, mature and dying 'ahinahina are found naturally, side by side. Park scientists and volunteers conduct a silversword count every summer to document the number of these resilient plants in the park.

The blooming season for 'ahinahina is May through October each year. An individual plant may be just a few years, or many decades, old before it blooms. What triggers a plant to bloom remains a mystery.

LAURENCE PARENT